*Leibniz, or The Best of All Possible Worlds*

To my son Joseph, this promise:
all is grace.

# Leibniz,
# or The Best of All Possible Worlds

Narrated by
Jean Paul Mongin

Illustrated by
Julia Wauters

Translated by
Jordan Lee Schnee

*Plato & Co.*
diaphanes

One by one, the lamps of grand Vienna were extinguished. The last of the people lingering in the narrow streets around the Hofburg, the seat of Austrian power, were on their way home to their beds. That spring night in 1714, a deep peace descended upon Schönbrunn Palace and the emperors' guard.

On the other side of the city, at the top of the oldest tower, a candle feebly lit walls that were covered by a marvelous library. It contained printed books and an even more impressive collection of manuscripts.

There were letters from the world's geniuses, works on mathematics, genealogical studies that stretched all the way back to prehistory, guides to strange languages, drawings of mechanical calculators, law texts, philosophical writings, even a few orders for secret missions. It was Gottfried Wilhelm von Leibniz's study.

This was an old man's domain, his friends and benefactors all long-departed. It was hard to see Leibniz's genius—one with few parallels in human history—in his melancholy appearance.

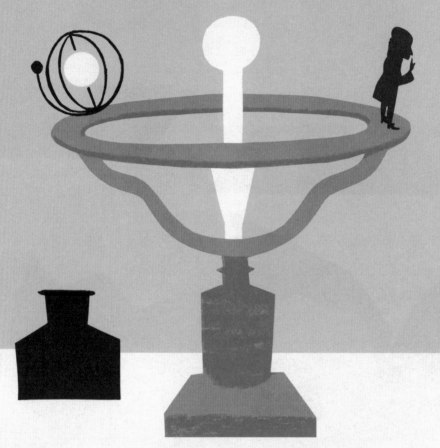

As a child, Leibniz had taught himself to read—not just his own language, but also Latin and Greek. He became a diplomat, and probably something of a spy. He had connections everywhere, from the Vatican to the Russian czar's court. An incredible genius, he was capable in all of the sciences of his time, even a bit ahead of them. All of this knowledge was hidden inside of a heavy, balding head supported with difficulty by his stooped body. Only his broad hands revealed old strength.

On this evening, the little old man took small sips from his stein of beer, savoring it as he awaited a visitor. He was holding a piece of paper covered in the same miniscule handwriting that was on 200,000 other sheets stuffed into his library. The ink was still drying. Leibniz had just completed his description of the universe.

"Objects," he wrote, "are made up of utterly simple substances: monads. Every monad is different, because each one is a point of view on the universe; and each one, as a small spiritual machine, goes from one point of view to another, according to the divine harmony that regulates change in the world. Thus, matter can perceive, can desire. Marble, for example, has its own ideas, albeit very confused ones."

A small step sounded on the stair. The old door opened
halfway, and a child with almond-shaped eyes slipped into
the study.

"Good evening, Mr. von Leibniz!" he said in a flute-like voice.

"Good evening my little Theodore," replied Leibniz without
turning around.

Theodore lived right at the foot of the tower where
Leibniz was residing. Before going to bed, he would
appear to say goodnight to the old philosopher,
hoping he would tell him a story.

Like every night, Leibniz asked him:
"So Theodore, what did you learn today?"
"I studied a poem by Virgil, and then after that my teacher told me the story of kings of Rome! How the Tarquin dynasty took power, the circus games, the defilement of the beautiful Lucretia, and then how they all killed each other!"
"And what do you think about all of that?" asked Leibniz.
"In the end the Tarquins were properly punished, but it would've been better to stop them earlier!"
"Oh really? But don't you think God could have stopped them earlier, if he had wanted to?"
"I don't know," said Theodore. "Maybe God didn't know that they were going to commit those crimes..."

"Theodore, do you really think that God, who is all-knowing, can overlook what his creatures are going to do?"

"I don't know! Maybe I could ask God right now if I'm going to move my right or my left foot, and then do the opposite of what he says: then he'd be wrong!"

Leibniz burst out laughing.

"I would rather think, my little Theodore, that God wouldn't answer you! Or maybe, if he answered, you'd be so awed that his prediction would become an order."

"But why then," said Theodore, "why didn't God command the Tarquins to be good kings? Or why didn't he choose another family to rule Rome?"

"Theodore, you've only known the world for a handful of days, and you find fault in it! You can barely see past the end of your nose. Wait until you know more, and, above all, consider the whole universe: you will see that it is unimaginably beautiful. You will find things there that you don't like one bit, but the world wasn't made for you alone—or rather, it was made for you if you become wise, and know how to recognize the great order underlying all the small disorders."

"Hmm. I don't get it," said Theodore sadly.

"So my boy, you know of the last of the Tarquins, the horrible Sextus Tarquinius, son of the king of Rome; the one who would commit the violation and murder of Lucretia. Imagine Sextus heading to Delphi to consult Apollo's oracle and learn of his destiny. The oracle delivers him this prophecy:

'Woe betide you, offspring of Tarquinius Superbus,
For when you become the king of Rome
You will violate Lucretia, misusing the throne,
Fallen and from your homeland banished,
Soon thereafter your life will vanish …'

Sextus Tarquinius appeals the oracle's announcement:
'I brought you a royal gift, O Apollo, and you tell me of
such a sad fate?'

*'Your riches are pleasing,'* responds Apollo's Oracle,
*'and I have done what you requested, informing*
*you of your fate. I can see the future*
*but I do not create it. Go complain to Jupiter,*
*king of the gods, and to the Fates who watch over*
*the paths of the stars and the destinies of humans.'*

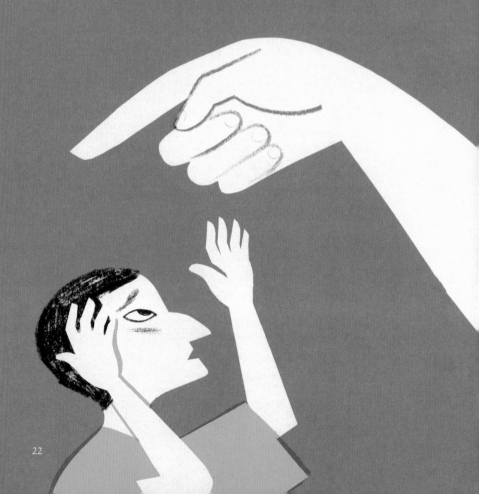

'I thank you, O holy Apollo, for showing me the truth. But on what grounds is Jupiter so cruel to me that he fixes such a harsh destiny for an innocent man?'

*'You, innocent?' laughs the oracle. 'Know that you will be vain, that you will be adulterous, that you will betray your country; and as Virgil says—don't try to change divine fate. My dear Sextus, the gods make everyone as they are: the rabbit is shy, the donkey dumb, the lion brave, the wolf predatory. Jupiter, king of the gods, has made your soul wicked and irredeemable. You will act according to your nature, and Jupiter will treat you as your actions merit. He swore that to Styx.'*

Leaving Apollo's temple at Delphi, Sextus goes to meet
Jupiter in his temple at Dodona, where the rustling of
the oak leaves conveys the king of the gods' message.
With the guidance of the temple's high priest, he presents
offerings and then lays out his complaint:
'Why have you condemned me, O great God, to be
evil, to be miserable?'

*'If you give up Rome,'* replies Jupiter, *'you will become
wise, you will become happy.'*

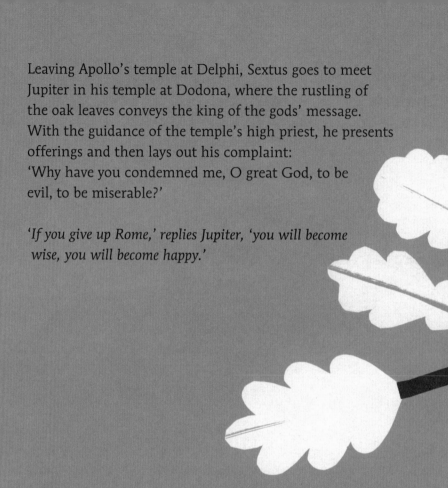

'Why must I renounce the crown?' replies Sextus,
'Could I not be a good king?'

*'No, Sextus. I know better what is right for you.
If you go to Rome, you are lost.'*

Sextus Tarquinius, who could not give up so much,
turns his back to the temple and surrenders to his fate.

In this story, the high priest of Jupiter is named Theodore, just like you. He's a lot like you. Witness to Sextus' confusion, he addresses the king of the gods himself: 'Your wisdom is beyond compare, O Jupiter! Sextus must recognize that his wretchedness is due only to his bad intentions! But your humble servant is surprised: he would admire your resoluteness just as he admires your greatness. Does it not depend on you that Sextus does not have better intentions?'

*'Go visit my daughter, Pallas Athena, goddess of wisdom. She will make you understand my work.'*

28

Theodore travels to Athens. He is told he should sleep in
Athena's temple, for she is Jupiter's daughter and the goddess
of wisdom. In his dreams, he is transported to an unknown
land. An unbelievably immense, shining palace appears.

The goddess Athena stands in the doorway, a corona of dazzling majesty around her. She is as beautiful and imposing as the poet Virgil says she is when she appears before the gods. She touches Theodore's face with an olive branch:

*'Jupiter, who loves you, recommended you come to me for guidance,' she says. 'This is the palace of destinies, which I protect. There are representations here, not only of what will happen, but all that is possible.'*

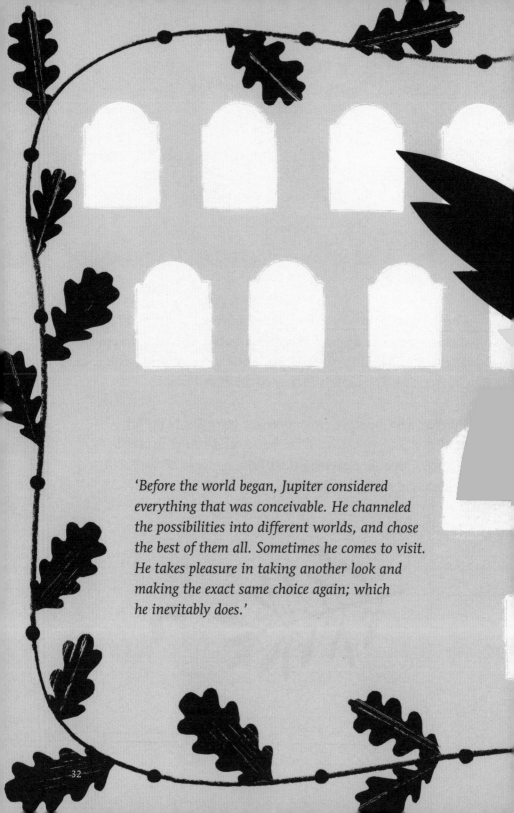

'Before the world began, Jupiter considered
everything that was conceivable. He channeled
the possibilities into different worlds, and chose
the best of them all. Sometimes he comes to visit.
He takes pleasure in taking another look and
making the exact same choice again; which
he inevitably does.'

'I just have to say the word,' continues the goddess, 'and we will see a world that my father could have created. Nothing would have been missing in it, but by changing just a miniscule thing in its story, we would see that a totally different world would come to pass.'

'Those worlds are all here in idea form. I will show you one where you will find one of the future Sextuses, and not the one that you just met. In one of these possible worlds, you will see a Sextus who is content and revered, in another a mediocre Sextus; still others hold Sextuses of all types and of infinitely many kinds.'

At that, the goddess leads Theodore into one of
the chambers: when he crosses the threshold,
it is not a chamber, but a world with its
own sun and stars.

At Athena's word, Jupiter's temple in Dodona appears. Sextus is leaving the temple, but in this world, we understand that he will obey the god's advice. We see him return to a city between two seas that looks like Corinth. He buys a small farm. While he is planting, he discovers treasure. He becomes a rich, well-loved, well-regarded man and dies at a ripe old age, cherished by his loved ones.

Theodore sees Sextus' whole life in a flash.
It is like a play.

This chamber is filled with a vast quantity of writings.
Theodore can not stop himself from asking what
they are for.

'That's the story of the world we just visited,' says the
goddess. 'It's the book of destiny. You saw a number on
Sextus' forehead. Look for the corresponding page in the book.
Put your finger on whichever line you choose, and you
will see appear in detail what the line outlines generally.'

Theodore does, and he sees all of the details of Sextus's life.

On into the next chamber, and there: another world, another book, another Sextus. He leaves the temple, resolved to obey Jupiter, and goes to Thrace. He marries the king's daughter. The king has no other children, so Sextus succeeds him. He is adored by his subjects.

In other rooms, there are always new scenes playing out.
The chambers are arranged in a pyramid. They become richer
and richer towards the top, and show worlds that are
increasingly beautiful.

Finally, the last chamber. It is the most beautiful of them
all, because the pyramid has an origin, but no visible end.
It has a summit, but does not really have a base, it grows and
grows towards infinity.

'That's because,' the goddess explains, 'among an
infinity of possible worlds, there is one that is the best.
If there weren't, Jupiter wouldn't have created
a single one. And each world has less perfect
worlds below it, this is why the pyramid of
possible worlds descends infinitely.'

Upon entering the final chamber, Theodore finds himself in ecstasy. Athena has to come to his aid: a drop of divine liqueur on his tongue revives him. He is overflowing with joy.

'*We are in the real world of today,*' *says the goddess,* '*and you are here at the source of happiness. This is what Jupiter has in store for you if you continue to serve him faithfully.*'

'And here is Sextus, as he is now, and as he will be. He leaves the temple in great anger. He disdains the Gods' advice. You can see him going to Rome, plunging the city into chaos, and injuring Lucretia, the wife of a friend. Now he is like his father: chased after, beaten, unhappy. If Jupiter had chosen a Sextus who was happy in Corinth, or king of Thrace, this wouldn't be the same world. At the same time, he could not have avoided choosing this world, the one more perfect than all the others, the pyramid's peak.

You see, Jupiter, king of the gods, did not make Sextus bad at all; he was eternally wicked, and it was always his choice. Jupiter only granted him existence, and in his wisdom could not reject the world which Sextus belonged to: he brought it from the realm of possibility into real existence.'

'Sextus's crime serves great purposes. It will give rise to an empire that will produce noble things. But that is nothing compared to the total value of this world, the beauty of which you are admiring now. Later, once you have gone on the pleasant journey from this mortal state to a better one, the gods will have made you able to understand it.

You already know that Jupiter is infinitely powerful. He is able to do anything, if he wills it. But you also know that he is infinitely good, that is to say he always wants the best. Now you see, every star, every leaf, every human —good or bad—every happy or sad event contributes to the world's perfection, and to the glory of the king of gods.'

Just then, Theodore wakes up. He gives thanks to the goddess, and understands Jupiter's justness. Moved by what he has just seen and understood, he continues being high priest with all the zeal of a true servant, and with all the bliss a mortal can muster."

Leibniz fell silent. His young companion's mind gently returned from the temple, where he was high priest of the king of gods, to the Viennese night.

Sextus Tarquinius

Sext

"If I'm able to visit the palace of destinies," said Theodore,
"I am going to ask how Jupiter is always able to recognize
Sextus! Because in one of the worlds he's good, and in the
other he's evil. In one, he's tall and strong, and in the other,
shrunken and hunchbacked. And maybe in some of the worlds,
Sextus isn't even born a Roman. In the end, you never know
who Sextus is!"

...uinius

Sextus Tarquinius

"That's because Sextus doesn't exist outside of the worlds he belongs to," answered Leibniz, "There is an infinity of Sextuses because there is an infinity of worlds that Sextus belongs to."

"As for you, Theodore, maybe you'll become an explorer, or a thief, or a great musician, or a businessman. God only knows! And you will be no less my little Theodore!"

"But it's not fair for Sextus Tarquinius! Because it was really God who made him a criminal and didn't save the best destiny for him!" protested Theodore.

"It's a bit like looking at a piece of organ music from the point of view of what one little tube will play. God didn't create Sextus to be a criminal. He created the world in which Sextus committed his crimes, because that was the most perfect world. Imagine that the world is a very beautiful work of art: each stroke of paint isn't the most beautiful color, but each makes the canvas more beautiful as a whole. Every pain, every mistake, contributes to the great order of the universe in the same way."

"Well if it's like that," said little Theodore, yawning, "then I should just stay in bed tomorrow, because God planned it like that, and this world is the best one."

"Or maybe, like in the story I told you, you will get up. You will give thanks to God and serve him faithfully, and he will fill you with joy! Because in truth, you don't know God's plan. That's why you should just do what is allotted to you, following the reasons God has provided you and the commandments he has given. If you do, your spirit will be at peace. Leave God to worry about success himself, because he will never miss doing the right thing, not only for the world as a whole, but also for you specifically—if you have real faith in him."

Leibniz waited for a smile to appear on his young friend's lips, then, very softly he added:

"My Theodore, won't you be the happiest of men if you learn to recognize an exquisite perfection in the world? You will see it all the better if you become a scholar, and study the stars or very tiny things. What's more, you will understand how the universe, in its entirety, goes far beyond the wisest intentions and reveals the goodness of its creator. The more the love of God catches fire within you, the more you will burn to imitate his divine justice in your own small ways. Then you will be like a little divinity of your own, one that is in a sense capable of society with God. And you will work with others to make up a divine city. The most perfect state ruled by the most perfect of princes."

The old philosopher got up painfully, then, drawn to the clear night sky, clomped over to the widow. He had always disdained astrology's fables, but sometimes the starry sky reminded him of the strange landscape drawn by the curves in his mathematical equations with their bottlenecks, their spirals, their points.

Meanwhile, Theodore listened to the sounds that filtered up to the study: soft household noises, sleepers' snores, nighttime conversations, wind in the alleyways ... Leibniz had once commented that he recognized the city's breathing that way, by not picking out any of the sounds that made it up. "It's because the ear," he had explained, "does addition with the tiny sounds without us being aware of it, and in this equation lies the secret of music." Theodore wondered if God enjoyed calculating possibilities to make worlds.

French edition:

*Leibniz ou le meilleur des mondes possibles*

Jean Paul Mongin & Julia Wauters

Design: Yohanna Nguyen

© Les petits Platons, Paris 2010

First edition

ISBN 978-3-0358-0142-2

© DIAPHANES, Zurich 2020

www.diaphanes.com

Layout: 2edit, Zurich

Printed and bound in Germany